W9-DFX-622

Adventures
TO IMAGINE

Thrilling Escapes in North America

BY PETER GUTTMAN

FODOR'S TRAVEL PUBLICATIONS, INC. • NEW YORK • TORONTO • LONDON • SYDNEY • AUCKLAND • WWW.FODORS.COM/

The publisher gratefully acknowledges Peter Guttman's contribution to the development of Fodor's "To Imagine" series.

Special Sales
Fodor's Travel Publications are available at special discounts for bulk purchases for sales promotions or premiums. Special editions, including personalized covers, excerpts of existing guides, and corporate imprints, can be created in large quantities for special needs. For more information, contact your local bookseller or Special Markets, Fodor's Travel Publications, 201 E. 50th Street, New York, NY 10022. Inquiries from Canada should be directed to your local Canadian bookseller or sent to Random House of Canada, Ltd., Marketing Dept., 1265 Aerowood Drive, Mississauga, Ontario L4W 1B9. Inquiries from the United Kingdom should be sent to Fodor's Travel Publications, 20 Vauxhall Bridge Road, London, England SW1V 2SA.

ISBN 0-679-00020-8
First Edition

PRINTED IN CHINA 10 9 8 7 6 5 4 3 2 1

Library of Congress Cataloging-in-Publication Data
Guttman, Peter, 1954–
Adventures to imagine: thrilling escapes in North America / by Peter Guttman—1st ed.
p. cm.
ISBN 0-679-00020-8 (alk. paper)
1. Outdoor recreation—United States—Guidebooks 2. Outdoor recreation—North America—Guidebooks. 3. United States—Guidebooks. 4. North America—Guidebooks. I. Title.
GV191.4.G88 1997
917.304'929—dc21 97-22529 CIP

While every care has been taken to ensure the accuracy of the information in this guide, time brings change, and consequently, the publisher cannot accept responsibility for errors that may occur. Call ahead to verify prices and other information.

Readers should also remember that adventure travel and outdoor vacations may entail certain risks. While outfitters, trip operators, and tour guides mentioned in this book have been carefully selected, the publisher makes no warranties regarding their competence, reliability, and safety practices and disavows all responsibility for injury, death, loss, or property damage that may arise from participation in their trips.

Acknowledgments
An eternal debt of gratitude is due to Fabrizio La Rocca for his wisdom, dedication, and infinite sense of balance.

Credits
Fabrizio La Rocca, Editor and Creative Director
Paula Consolo, Text Editor
Allison Saltzman, Designer
Jolie Novak, Editorial Assistant

Enthusiastically dedicated to my radiant soul mate, Lori, for helping set the sails towards the winds of adventure, and to Chase, for promising a dazzling sunrise just beyond the horizon.

CONTENTS

Imagine living life at full tilt, your spirits soaring through the fast lane at speeds well off the radar screen. Shifting gears in the breeze, you catch a swirling vista of wonder and curiosity racing past the windshield. Childhood fascination spills out of the glove compartment, as you leave a discarded set of rusty, jaded attitudes trailing in the exhaust. Forging your days into high-octane adventures requires a knack most of us can develop in the nick of time. Seeking out new terrains of experience, we can push the envelope and ensure our souls do not grow gray before our hair does.

I vividly recall my first wildlife safari—collecting backyard fireflies in a bottle. Even now I can taste the exhilarating freedom of the morning my dad removed the training wheels from my bike, let go of the seat, and watched me solo around an empty parking lot, soon destined to explore the more remote, exotic fringes of my neighborhood. In a quantum leap of faith, I parachuted out of a single engine plane to commemorate my college graduation day.

Ever since, whether swimming with sharks in Bora Bora, lodging with retired headhunters in Borneo, or stretching to reach Earth's zenith by climbing a radar mast at the North Pole, I have treasured a simple truth: Enthusiasm is a currency far more valuable than gold. I suppose that's why I've always been more concerned with crafting a life than making a living.

Fortunately, jump-starting a career in exhilaration does not necessitate changing your whole latitude. Beckoning just down the street and in our own backyard, the North American continent is a colossal unfenced adventureland that offers an astonishing variety of wildlife, landscapes, and recreational exploits. Here I have answered the call of the wild by mushing my own dog team through a wintry fairy-tale forest, been sucked into a cat and mouse dodgeball game with farm belt tornados, wormed my way through skinny subterranean chambers lit only by my headlamp, and felt the barnacles and affectionate curiosity of monstrous gray whales emerging from the warmth of a desert lagoon.

Many of these snapshots required a certain willingness to throw comfort, convenience, and sometimes even caution to the wind. It's easy to forget how we've evolved in just a few short generations; a pioneer culture that had to endure covered wagon hardships in search of distant homelands is now an automobile culture that endures traffic jams in search of parking spots nearest the local shopping mall entrance.

In this air-bagged society of risk aversion, it often seems easier to experience our thrills vicariously. Television, video games, and the Internet might offer a safe refuge from the daily humdrum, but they artificially shelter us in a numbing virtual reality where real life seems to hold little virtue. Surfing is more likely to involve a couch-anchored tap of the index finger than a wet encounter with nature's awesome forces, and we've moved to climbing corporate ladders rather than mountain precipices.

I strongly believe the desire for youthful vitality, the quest for cutting-edge novelty, and the urge for hypercaffeinated thrills is deeply ingrained in the American character. When letting go of life's handrails, we confront our fears and find all our senses starting to operate on heightened alert. We're compelled to explore the undiscovered edges of our own limits, guaranteeing that life is never treated like merely a dress rehearsal.

This is an escapist scrapbook of those magical fantasies I've cooked up over the years. It includes some soothing activities for tanning your soul as well as an all-American red carpet invitation to white knuckle, blue-in-the-face thrills. Whether a meditative Walter Mitty type or a gung ho Indiana Jones, you'll find these pages will quench your thirst for adventure. But, be forewarned of adrenaline's addiction; you might wake up in a cold sweat lusting for just a small fix of what's brewing over the horizon—a refreshing gulp of more adventures to imagine.

Peter Guttman
New York, 1997

Mountain Biking

the Slickrock Trail

The red rock country of Utah's lonely outback is a mountain biker's mecca, a slice of geologic casserole known as the Colorado Plateau. Bumping down steep flights of rocky stairs and pogo-sticking your way across surreal landscapes of domes, fins, and petrified sand dunes is like riding a paint-shaking machine. Breezes wipe your sweaty brow, your legs pumping out precision grunt work, as you aspire to quick and seamless downshifts on an intricate assembly of cogged gears. Keep up a satisfying, shock-absorbing momentum, while surfing undulating waves of parched, ruby slick-rock. Swooping into deep stone bowls, use speed to propel your bike up and over the next slope. Negotiate sand traps by shifting your weight, and veering off the trail across soaring stone bridges, you carefully guide fat tires along narrow ledges. To maintain control, feather your brakes as you whirl by tadpole-filled potholes. With an assortment of tools and an adequate supply of thirst-quenching liquids, you return from the desert's jagged edges, exhilarated from this bone-jarring rodeo on wheels.

Tall Ship

Sailing

on the trade winds of the Caribbean

Windswept from an earlier gilded age, the S.Y. *Sea Cloud* plows through churning waves to the next exotic port of call. Like out of a frame of *Mutiny on the Bounty*, acres of canvas scoop gusts and blossom, stretching from four masts that soar higher than church steeples. On the world's tallest mainmast, a congestion of deckhands scramble high above teak and mahogany decks, wrestling on the yardarms with a stubborn immensity of billowing fabric. Taut sails are nimbly set by muscular arms working in choreography, as ropes are neatly coiled around shiny brass belays. With an officer's permission, you assist with some of the lines and perhaps ascend the swaying mizzenmast, making certain to fasten your safety harness onto a jackstay. Later, slump into the netting at the end of a sixty-foot bowsprit and feel the mighty windjammer buck beneath the creaking rigging. A pod of dolphins rides the ship's currents, seemingly racing the hand-carved eagle figurehead. In rhythm with the sea's rolls and pitches, sailors' chanteys waft from crew quarters below and softly fill the salt-sprayed evening.

Wagon Train Pioneering

along the Oregon Trail

Wagon's ho! Creaking along in stubborn convoys, waves of pioneer emigrants once swept across the rugged American heartland. Today, starkly silhouetted crumbs of eroding mountain signpost the hot and dusty Oregon Trail, where wagon ruts still etch arid rattlesnake territory. Brushing the cactus thorns from your boots, you grease the overburdened axles, hitch the horses, and hop into your prairie schooner as its wooden wheels bounce across the Nebraska vastness. On the horizon, ballooning cloud castles spawn violent hailstorms, then dissolve into rainbows that lasso distant mesas. In the shadows of Chimney Rock, you set a course toward the sinking sun along an undulating plateau and into shaded canyons. An oasis of perfumed pines and wild roses provides a comfortable evening camp. With wagons circled to corral the livestock, buffalo hump roasts slowly in an earthen pit, while vinegar pudding and hoecakes steam in cast-iron kettles. When the eerie howls of hungry coyotes subside, you bed down beyond the campfire, a harmonica rhapsody as lullaby.

Stranded by mud in Canada's Bay of Fundy, Seal Cove's clutch of fishing boats slowly regain their buoyancy. Boarding a chartered craft, you ride the tides past seaweed-edged shoreline until the faint silhouette of a lighthouse emerges from the ocean mist. The shrill cacophony of an avian society announces the 15-acre Machias Seal Island. You shuttle in by tender and scramble the guano-slicked ramp, cautiously making your way across the sedge, where annoyed Arctic terns patrol their eggs. Moving quickly, protect your head with a hat and bird stick, waving off the frightening dive-bomb attacks. From a small wooden observation shelter, you peer out on a thriving Atlantic puffin community, gathered in the thousands at their southernmost nesting site. These clownlike birds, often considered penguins of the north, stack silver herring in their bright orange beaks for fast-food delivery to nests just feet from your spying binoculars. In a few short weeks, the sad-eyed sea parrots will terminate their summer occupation and whir across the Atlantic toward Iceland.

Puffin Birding

on Machias Seal Island

Houseboating

around Lake Powell

Houseboating through the forked gorges of Glen Canyon is like entering an intoxicating daydream torn from the pages of Mark Twain. It's a real chart house challenge to pilot an ungainly shoe box of a craft through this intriguing jigsaw puzzle of red rock and jade water. Tie up at a remote canyon beach to explore the remains of millennium-old cave dwellings. As the desert heats up, retrieve your fishing rod and seek the shade of an immense overhanging cathedral of Navajo sandstone. From the back deck, launch the kayak for a solitary paddle. Each bend reveals a hanging garden of flowering cactus, as the sinking sun splashes a golden shellac across miles of corrugated terrain. Slowly, you navigate the boat through trenches that slash an intimidating one-way passage down rocky vaults striped by eons of geologic history. Pastels bloom in the dusky sky as you pull into Cathedral Canyon's secret cove and await the dance performance of constellations swirling across the wilderness night.

A century ago, hungry livestock were driven across huge avenues of unfenced western prairie by the stoic lonesome cowboy. Today, you can ride as hired hands alongside those mythic legends, trafficking herds into obedient patterns through the Thompson River valley. Galloping steeds and clopping hooves discharge clouds of dust along an endless Montana range. High in the Rockies, near the Continental Divide, cattle drives

Cattle Driving

move in rhythm with the season's pasture growth. During this ten-mile day riding high in your saddled bully pulpit, you duck branches and dodge cow pies, funneling rambunctious strays with a nimble equine gait. Common horse sense and whooshing lariats do the trick when whoops and whistles fail to dislodge wayward bulls from their comfort zones. The bellowing bovine finally leave their summer camp and file back to the ranch, where six-shooter vaccine guns await their return and grilled steaks reward you and your fatigued fellow wranglers.

Roundups *in Big Sky country*

Tornado Chasing *across the Great Plains*

Unique on this planet, tornado alley is the flattened immensity of plains visited each May by enemy weather fronts poised to do battle. Storm chasers, armed with road maps, laptop weather charts, and an exquisite instinct for reading severe skies, vie for front-row seats to one of nature's most striking

spectacles. On this determined race across a checkerboard of blowing wheat and corn-fields, you arrive at the target area to hunt for a dry line boundary, marking the place where the Gulf's sultry air streams into moisture-drained Arctic forces. Your caravan speeds toward floating mountains of boiling cumulo-nimbus vapor, soon twice the height of Everest and tinted garish shades of turquoise and mango. Sizzling shards of brilliant lightning slice the prairie as you deploy the hail guard to minimize damage from golf ball-size stones that pound percussively onto your vehicle. Core-punching the storm's center, position yourself for southwesterly escape options, while overhead a brooding wall cloud begins to pirouette. As winds scream and a whirling spindle of energy descends to scrape the earth, you enter a state of terror, with more than a feeling you're not in Kansas anymore.

Harp Seal Viewing

among Gulf of St. Lawrence ice floes

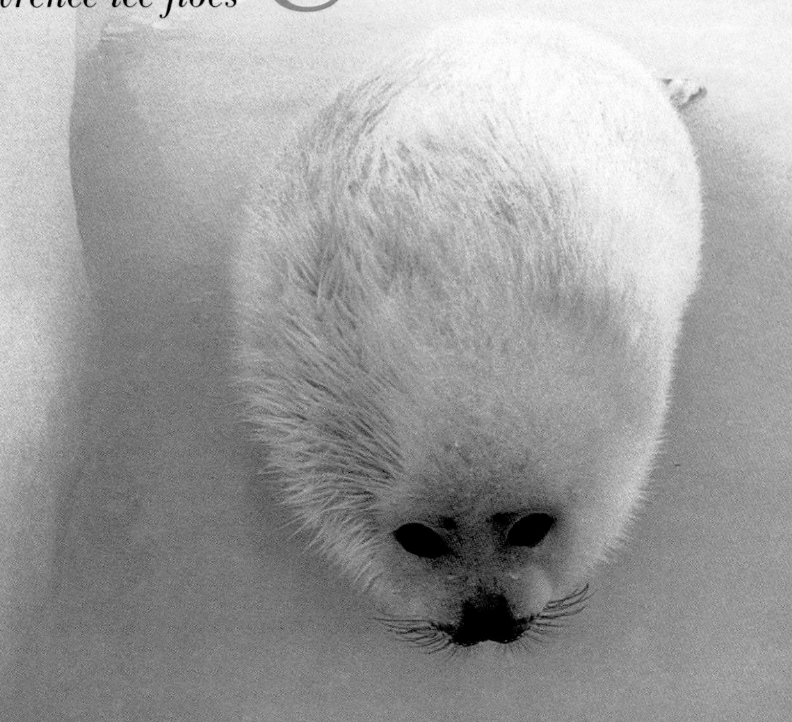

Caked pans of wind-driven ice clog the shallow waters of the Gulf of St. Lawrence, virtually the only place on earth where you can pay a home visit to the harp seal. Your flotation-equipped helicopter judders down into the frozen nursery, filled with the commotion of grunting males, whimpering pups, and the territorial barking of overly concerned mothers. Guided by former seal hunters, you tread gingerly with cleated boots, using a staff to probe for dangerous crevices in the splintered surface. At your feet white-coated pups display a vulnerable innocence, accentuated by their searching, soulful eyes. In the lee of an opalescent pressure ridge, their sausage-shaped bodies melt the ice beneath them, creating snug cradles where they await mom's return from nearby blowholes. Choppering into another frigid neighborhood, you visit more cantankerous hooded seals and their blueback pups slithering across the ice. Be wary of the balloonlike inflation of their nostrils, a signal of their displeasure and a reminder that in this frozen galaxy of seals, you are only a temporarily tolerated visitor from another world.

Cloaked in a fire resistant suit, hooded by a padded brain bucket, and harnessed into a five-point safety belt, you feel like a cannon about to be lit. Scrunching into the single seat of a wide-wheeled, four-cylinder, two-liter, 125-horsepower Scandia Formula 2000, with your rear end just inches above the pavement, removes all doubt. A baritone rumble erupts with a pull on the ignition switch and a press of the starter button. You grip the wildly responsive steering wheel; throw your gears with a short, snappy motion; and weave through a sequence of turns, maximizing your time on full throttle. With elbows pressed in toward your body, the perfect heel-toe gymnastics of braking and downshifting buys you an instant to glance at the tachometer and plan your angle of attack on the next rapidly approaching bend. This hyper-kinetic carousel evolves into a slow-motion blur of raceway scenery, which stops only when the checkered flag snaps you out of your trance and back into the pit.

Race Car Driving

in the Poconos

Portaging

the Seven Carries of Saint Regis Canoe Area

In the northern Adirondacks, the Arctic ice shield left in its wake an exquisite wilderness pockmarked by deep depressions filled with glacial melt. This string of liquid pearls provided fur trappers easy paddling access to the interior mountains. The remaining network of canoe carries stitches together a series of distinct riparian worlds. Gliding across Little Clear Pond as an opaque curtain of morning mist ascends, you spot osprey fishing in the shallows near banks of wild cranberries. Blue darning needles flit along the shore, where beavers munch a lone birch amid thick groves of conifer. At the landing, piggyback your craft over a forested boardwalk and then drop into a meandering tributary of Saint Regis Pond. Here the bloodshot leaves of carnivorous pitcher plants fringe a spongy bog, where in the wrong season, their daily intake of insects seems woefully inadequate. Beneath the crenellations of the Sentinel Range, you pick a pocket-sized island for your tent as loons skitter across the glassy waters and prepare for their nocturnal laments.

Climbing the slope of Mt. Van Hoevenberg, you catch an unrecognizable blink-of-an-eye blur of red and hear a chorus of frightening shrieks. At the starting gate, a training Olympic bobsled driver jams you into a bulletlike eight-foot-long capsule, wrapping your legs over another passenger. A brakeman jump starts gravity with a strenuous running push, and your sled rockets down a frozen glass-smooth tube gleaming like an icicle. The horizon flips at whiplash speeds as you climb walls and bank steep curves in a roaring 800-pound Flexible Flyer. Under your helmet, quivering cheek muscles migrate into your ear, as g-forces double and your eyeballs swirl like fighter jets in a video game. Screaming blades scalp the tracks and your thirty-something-second journey leaves you completely toasted on this widely acknowledged champagne of thrills—the only bobsled run in North America.

Olympic Bobsledding

at Lake Placid

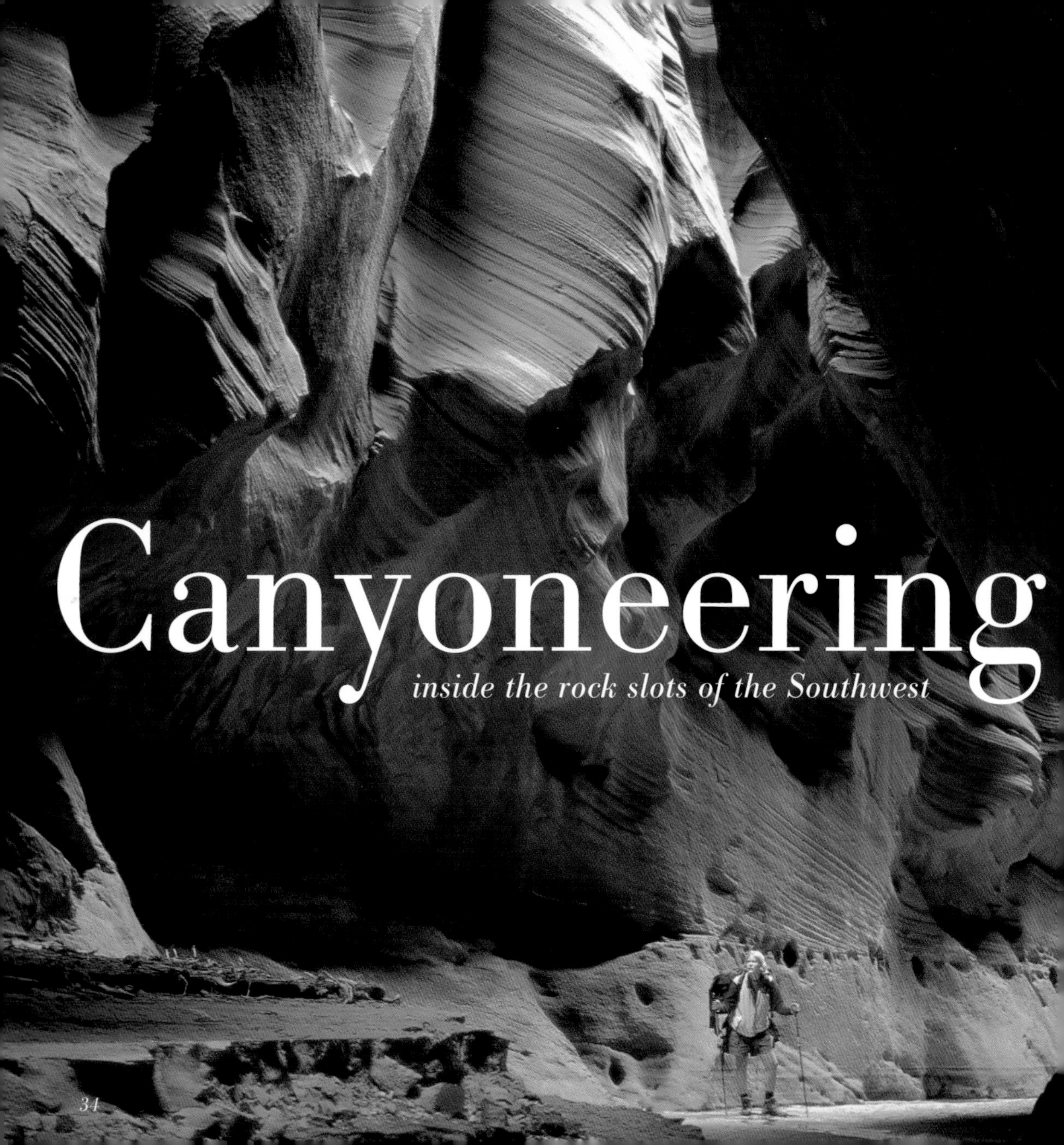

Canyoneering

inside the rock slots of the Southwest

Gaining access into some of the most wondrous landscapes on earth often requires the Herculean skills needed in a triathlon—weightlifting, hiking, and swimming. Before entering the narrow rock slots that slice a thousand feet below the Utah-Arizona border, check the forecast and rule out the probability of flash floods, which can roar down the skinny corridors leaving few escape routes. You slip into neoprene booties to reduce the risk of overexposure in the chilly depths of the Buckskin Gulch tributary and prepare to float your sixty-pound pack across deep, plunge-pool grottoes. This is an unrelenting boot camp for your prune-like feet, sloshing through prismatic globs of shoe-sucking quicksand for several ten-hour days. Swirls of flowing stone glow in the brief splashes of sunlight that manage to filter through steep side gorges. Hidden trails lead toward awesome natural arches swimming with lizards and into verdant oases of lush vegetation, where unmarked campsites provide an aromatic scorpion-free patch for slumber. Lights out when the full moon slips behind canyon walls.

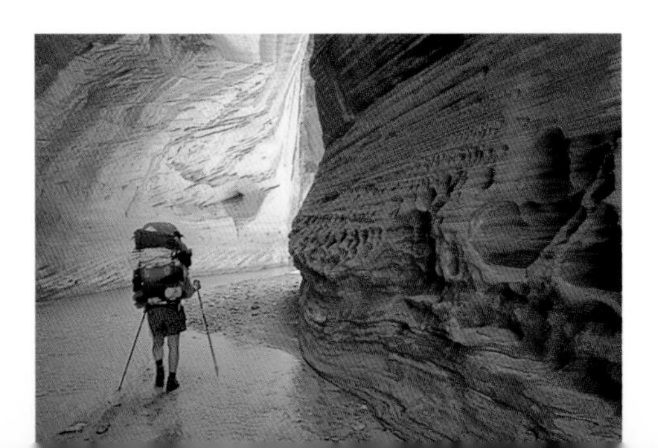

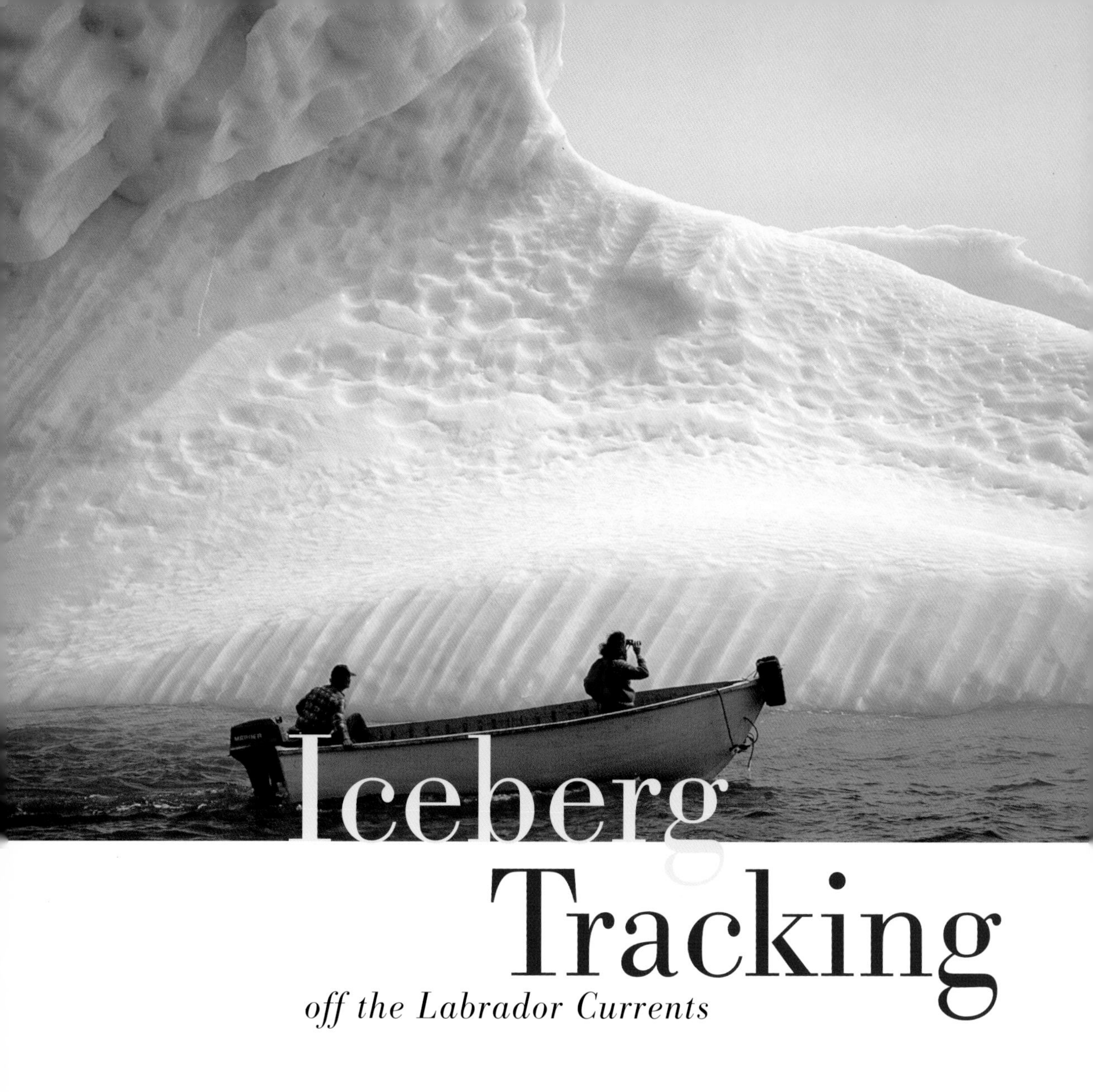

Iceberg Tracking

off the Labrador Currents

Though it's not always possible to journey to distant lands, by cleverly positioning yourself distant lands may sometimes journey to you. During late spring, in the tidy fishing outport of Twillingate, a frozen chunk of Greenland's far off coastline nudges into the crowded tickles of the Newfoundland peninsula. Torn from glacial sheets melting thousands of miles away at the edge of the polar ice cap, enormous growlers and smaller bergy bits transit iceberg alley, where the *Titanic* met its deep-freeze destiny. Board a chartered vessel or local fishing dory and set a course for the drifting turquoise mountains, eroded into dazzling sculpture and glimpsed on the horizon. Murres and shearwaters glide overhead and the temperature plunges as you approach the rendezvous. Keep a cautious distance from these refrigerated monoliths, relatively stable for the past 12,000 years but now rapidly melting, threatening to catapult into capsizing waves. Back at the dock, celebrate nature's harsh beauty with a sailor's whiskey on ice, the berg's explosively popping cubes, which are chipped, bagged, and sold here in quaint village stores.

Rolls of vibrant fabric are pulled, yanked, and filled with air, as scores of balloons prepare for mass ascension. You hurdle a suede-trimmed basket, congested with stainless steel propane tanks, instrument panel, and the high hopes of eager passengers and pilot. A tug on the blast handle ignites fiery jets that shoot buoyant warmth deep into a colossal nylon envelope, bulging with almost 100,000 cubic feet of air. Tethers are released and your wicker container eases you up, up and away from the fairgrounds, over the waving crowds, who turn increasingly Lilliputian. Villages become a collection of doll-houses, as an array of aerial ornaments hangs across the curving horizon. You eye the altimeter. Periodic blasts of hissing flames enable the balloon to hitch a ride with the appropriate currents and float like a bubble, at one with the wind. There is never a breeze and only spectacular silence. Watch for livestock and power lines as you descend onto fields for an evening's communal celebration of incandescent glow.

Hot Air Ballooning

over the Green Mountains

Climbing *atop the South Peak of Seneca Rocks*

Threatening to pierce the sky with its Tuscarora sandstone knife edge, 900-foot Seneca Rocks is a magnet for rock jockeys seeking the sheerest walls east of the Mississippi. Ready to defy gravitational forces and a skeptical nervous system, you adjust your sticky climbing shoes and begin the search for dime-thick ledges on which to support yourself. Tied in with aluminum snap-link anchors, wedging nuts, and odd widgets, you observe as your leader grapples to slip a life-supporting chock into a tiny crevice. With body twisted at improbable angles, you struggle to maintain both your center of equilibrium and a relaxed positive attitude, while jamming fingernails into slivers of cracks and denying the vertiginous abyss below. Tiptoeing up a precipice is a matter of crystallized will and chesslike strategy. Finally perched on God's antenna, savor the exhilaration and collect your wits: it's time for a summit plummet—rappelling off the edge in a smoothly controlled movement that walks you down the cliff face and eventually lowers you into an ecstatic embrace with terra firma.

Among the most mysterious environments on earth, the Everglades yields its grandeur only to the patient observer. Easing your canoe into the Turner River, you drift downstream with faint winds that comb strands of Spanish moss against branches of cypress. Paddle quietly through a corkscrewing maze of mangrove alleyways, and pause to watch an osprey take flight across a Jurassic saw grass prairie. In this ecologically

Canoeing Swamp

fragile kingdom of Disneyesque nature tableaux, snakes drape tree limbs and downed logs serve as launching pads for turtles. You inch toward the gulf through salt marshes where fiddler crabs jitterbug away from scavenging pelicans. Alligator-infested sloughs open into shallow saltwater bays teeming with bottlenose dolphins. When you reach your wooden chickee, slip into a protective netted evening gown to thwart the ambition of hungry mosquitoes, who usually have the last word with unprepared campers.

Trails *through the Everglades*

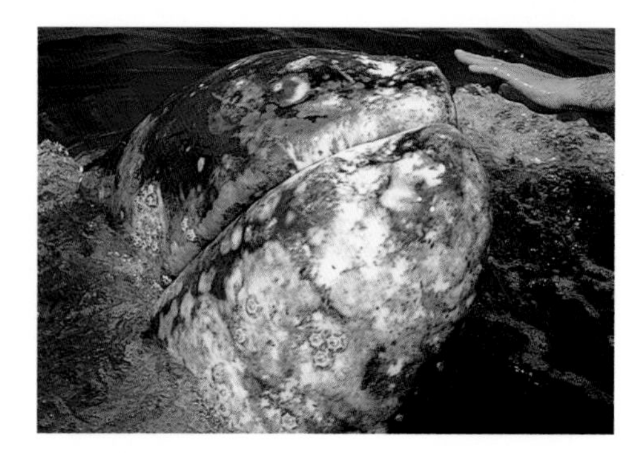

The greatest migratory marathon of any mammal is the 5,000-mile commuter run of the gray whale. After dining in the chilly Bering Sea, these leviathans find their way into the bathtub-warm safety of Baja's hidden lagoons, their watery maternity ward. A tightly formed squadron of pelicans glide toward the sculpted dunes, while distant grays hoist their 150 tons of blubber into periscope formation. The friendly whales maneuver closer to your boat and signal their intention to dock with a pungent exhalation: a rainbow of mucus and salt water sprayed across the bow. The panga's idling engines lure the nursing newborns with riveting vibrations. Easily the size of ten elephants, a protective mama emerges from the emerald surface, bumping the fishing vessel with a few playful Jonah-invoking swats of her flipper. Peering into the intelligent soul beneath those baseball-size eyes, you find it difficult to resist the temptation to plant a kiss on that beautiful barnacle-encrusted jowl.

Whale Kissing *inside San Ignacio Lagoon*

Land Yachting

across the Mojave Desert

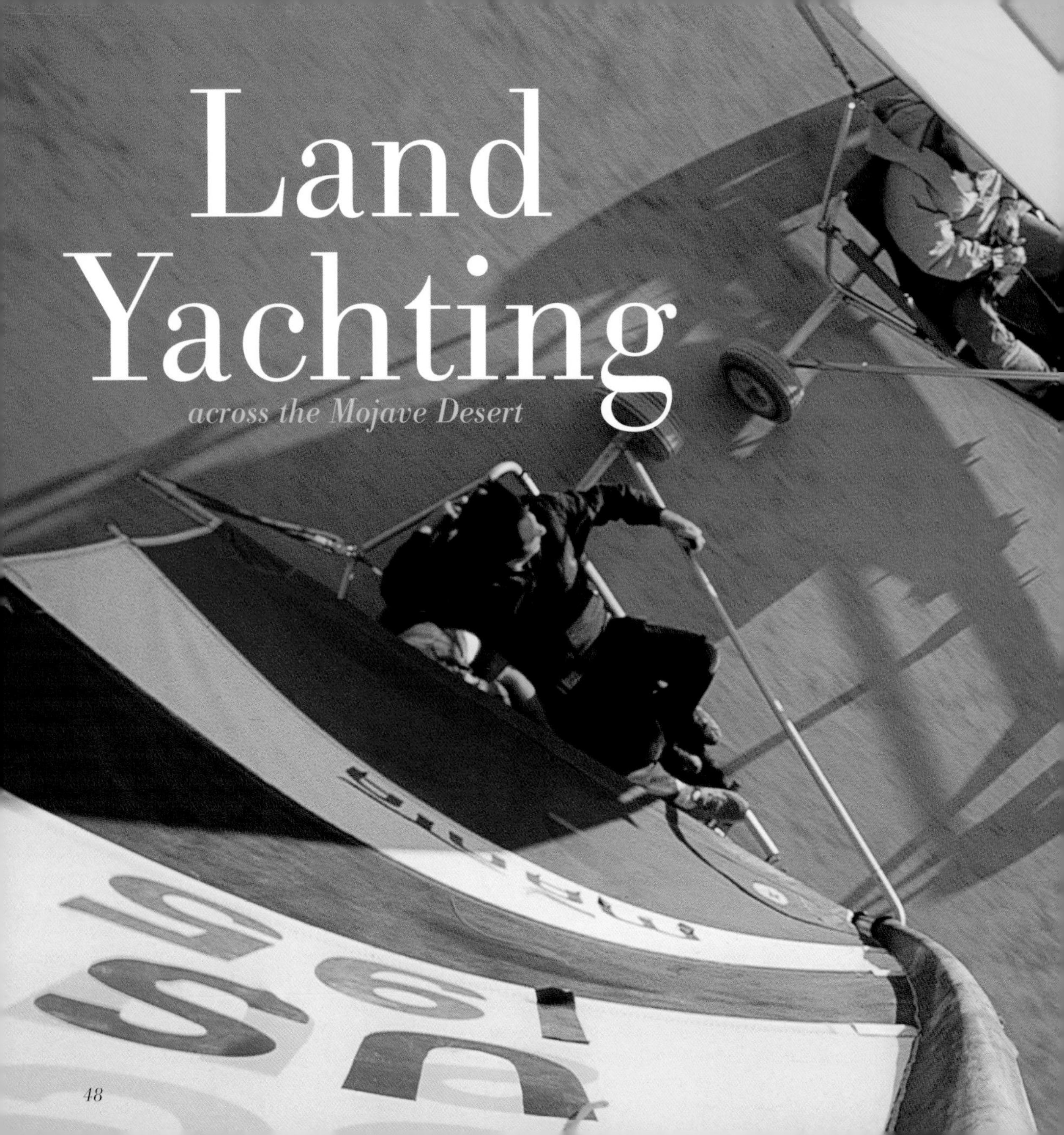

On the cracked, baked expanses of El Mirage Dry Lake, tumbleweed races toward the distant Shadow Mountains powered by blasts of scorched air. Hitching a daredevil ride on these winds, a fleet of colorful land yachts flies across the uninterrupted barrens chasing the horizon's mirage. Belted into a bucket seat and steering with your feet, you capture runaway gusts in the mainsail while the cement-hard ground slides beneath you at more than sixty miles per hour. Golden plumes of dust are fired up as you reverse directions and the three-wheeled contraption teeters at precarious angles. Should you tire of wafting across this moonscape like an errant dandelion spore, let out your sail and steer into the blowing currents. These sailing vehicles are an updated version of turn-of-the-century wind wagons, which transported workers and equipment to remote desert gold mines. They cavort in casual competitions till sundown, when the nighttime racing venue is monopolized by scores of kangaroo rats chased by hungry predators.

US
557

195

95
42
MANTA
manta

Encountering Polar Bears

in the Arctic tundra

In the wilds of northern Manitoba, Arctic fox and flightless ptarmigan struggle against the fierce boreal winds ripping across white-capped Hudson Bay. Here at these hunting grounds, hundreds of polar bears gather each autumn, eagerly anticipating the opening of their frozen cafeteria. The ferocious snow-white carnivores, peeved by their meager summer diet, wait for the bay to freeze, then station themselves at the breathing holes maintained by ringed seals throughout winter. You can lumber into this highly charged ecosystem in a tundra buggy, whose oversize tires carry you high enough to escape the powerful swipe of razor-sharp claws. Shotgun-wielding scouts safeguard your arctic safari and discourage unruly ursine behavior. Extend your stay for an overnight if tundra fever sets in, and bunk down in what amounts to an inverted zoo. Safely encased behind your metal cage, you feed on prime rib, while outside, curious black noses nuzzle at the frosted window panes.

In the Helderberg range of upstate New York, a series of low hills sit astride an immense layer of Onondaga limestone. Hidden by woods of hemlock and oak, a stone porthole serves as hatchway into the subterranean universe. There is precious little room to funnel through, so leave your claustrophobia and a clean change of clothes behind. With a chin-strapped helmet, knee pads, and at least three sources of illumination, you shimmy down into a slippery dark chamber polished by dripping moisture and an underground waterway. Vertical ledges of calcite create a delicate rimrock dam. In the cave's eternal 48 degrees, you stave off hypothermia by wearing layers but still must prepare for worming through eleven-inch-high crawlways that cleave chamber walls 60 feet below the planet's surface. Your beaming carbide lamp catches the echoing wing beats of brown bats, and as you belly-slither your way through 4,800 feet of terrestrial cavity, you lust for fresh air and light at the end of the tunnel.

Spelunking

under Albany County

Heli-
ALPINE
Alpine

Hiking

through the Purcell Range

In the distance, a tympanic crescendo of avalanches echoes across the Canadian Rockies' remote chain of mountains. Deposited by helicopter near a 9,000-foot summit, you bushwhack down a steep slope to Anemone Lakes, passing moose-trimmed greenery and waves of orange Indian paintbrush. Milky, silt-laden streams spill into sun-dappled glacial tarns, while marmots scurry through deposits of scree. As crushed slate tinkles under your feet, try to avoid holes engineered by grizzly bears sniffing for a pika meal. Blades dancing peak to peak, your aerial limousine then drops you onto Conrad Glacier, where you take care to sidestep pools sculpted by spinning rocks and treacherous fissures that cut 150 feet into the icy bowels. Up above, the jet-powered whirlybird buzzes across the moraine and, with Swiss efficiency, returns for its weary human cargo. The intense suction of swirling rotors almost vacuums the wet pants from your legs. Hunker down into a heli-huddle, your entire group crouching in an earthbound anchor. Back at an isolated lodge, a masseuse prepares you for another day of cheating gravity.

In the ecologically rich environment of an ancient sierra, the Smoky Mountains link up with the Blue Ridge chain. Under the Paleozoic shadows of Salt Rock, you meet and sniff your hairy camping partners in the soupy mist of Pisgah National Forest. Carefully, you balance the llamas' stuff sacks, grab the lead rope, and head down the valley trail. With an amusing touch of aristocracy, the animals saunter in a procession across the narrow log bridges that span Panthertown Creek. These tireless fuzzy station wagons bear the substantial weight of camping gear and dining supplies. You stride with a purpose through a lengthy thicket of rhododendron, interrupted only by the occasional path of red fox. Arriving at Schoolhouse Falls, duck behind a hissing curtain of fern-soaking spray to shower before dinner. Hors d'oeuvres and elaborate salads are washed down with white wine—an unexpected epicurean touch to this oddball back-country scene, where an outdoor seat is guaranteed and the Muzak is replaced by the screams of distant bobcats.

Llama Trekking

across the Smokies

Reenacting Historic Battles

in a Pennsylvania cornfield

Dawn seeps across the dewy meadow. Subtly, the fragrance of wood fires and horse manure tinges the morning chill, as syncopated tones of snoring emanate from dog tents carpeting acres of rolling farmland. Suddenly, a bugler's brassy notes summon legions of soldiers into assembly. Men grab their gear, stuff hardtack and ammunition into haversacks, and stomp off in parade ground precision to a rendezvous with opposing forces. Crouching low, you use your teeth to rip open packets of black powder, ram it down your rifle barrel, and await orders from a white-gloved captain. Volley after deafening volley of gunfire echoes across open fields, as hilltop cannons engage in a punishing duel for supremacy. Perspiring under an afternoon sun inside an itchy woolen uniform, you storm wooden fences while dodging explosions and fighting heat exhaustion. All across the valley, the thunderous power of stampeding cavalry is unleashed, and when the clouds of gunpowder clear, thousands lie motionless in the mud.

Dogsledding

on Minnesota's Boundary Waters

Out on the glassy surface of Horseshoe Lake, steamy clouds of canine breath signal the team's imminent departure. The iron-clawed snow hook is released, and the crossbred animals hurl instinctively into a rhythmic, tail-wagging gallop, their eager paws pounding the frozen pond. In dogged pursuit of the distant forested shoreline, the huskies try to outrun their gangline's harness. Entering the woods, the barking freight train barrels down the historic Banadad logging trail. Guard your face as you race between splayed limbs of evergreen, burdened under its snowy mantle. Mushing toward a treacherously banked slope, work the foot brakes with your moose-hide mukluks, leaning on one runner to keep from smacking stumps and executing an unscheduled somersault over the handlebars. Having weathered wipeouts that almost unhinged overnight gear stuffed into the canvas-covered cargo holds, you unload at your destination, a yurt's cozy pocket of warmth. Outside, the staccato rasp of tired, bawling animals ricochets across the wilderness, as faraway wolves mirror their cries in a primal chorus.

Tucked deep within the remote mountain folds of West Virginia's Monongahelas, the Upper Gauley River plunges madly in drops of up to ten feet, creating one of North America's premiere stretches of white water. Rafting this maelstrom, an obstacle course of tractor-size boulders, requires keen concentration and team effort. Shouting over the deafening roar, your guide issues urgent stroking directions to you and your crew—six tightly wedged oarsmen in wet suits, life jackets, and helmets. Soon your inflatable raft lunges violently into hydraulic depressions and boat-munching holes, and you are drenched in spray and adrenaline. Keep your eye on the next seething cauldron; avoid it or the rubber crafts will be coughing up swimmers into pounding eight-foot waves. Up ahead, chunks of sandstone from cliffs high above camouflage Class V rapids and tricky eddies that might flush into rocky cul de sacs. With steady nerves and honed navigational skills, slide through narrow shoots and into effervescent waters that slam you, finally, toward your take-out.

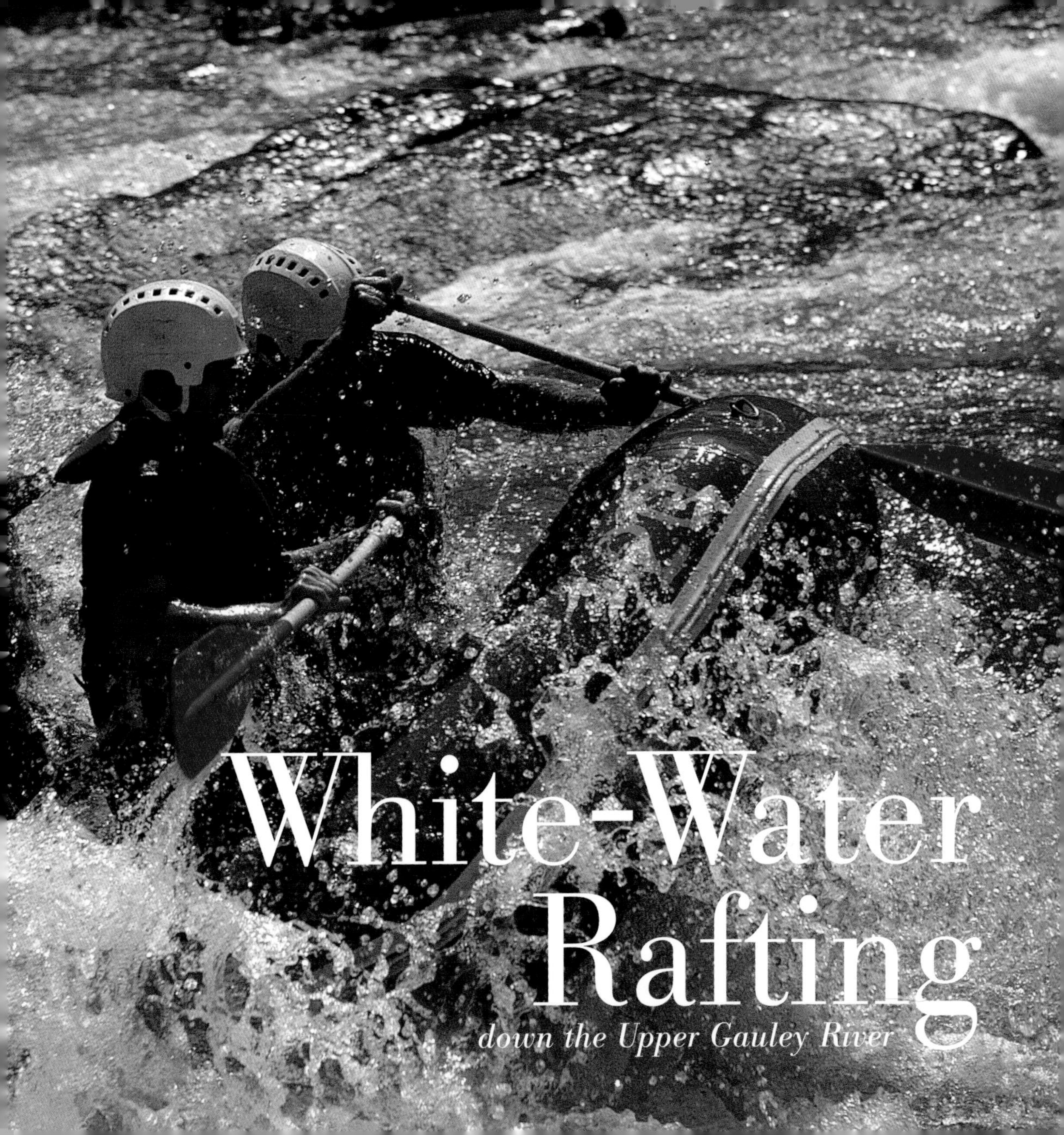

White-Water Rafting

down the Upper Gauley River

Hiking Hut to Hut

atop the White Mountains

The high-altitude trails of New England's White Mountains sew together a series of back-country huts, spaced apart by only a day's worth of worn boot leather. Saved from the burden of shouldering overnight supplies, you fill a day pack for a spectacular, ridge-clinging shuttle to the next dormitory-style stone shelter. Leaving Madison Spring's dramatic mountain col setting, you skirt glacial tarns and quartz-encrusted formations near the Knife Edge. Dress adequately to hike toward the windswept zenith at Lakes of the Clouds Hut, where, even in warmer months, you could encounter some of the world's worst weather. Approaching levels of meteorological absurdity, sudden thunderstorms, ferocious gales, and pounding hailstorms smash the region, and the fog thickens enough to give tall hikers a difficult time seeing their own feet. The harsh micro-climates produce snowy pygmy forest, where the stingy sun prods delicate wildflowers into bloom. Hares dart through the krummholz, and juncos flirt with the lower elevations. There, richly carpeted grounds of spongy sphagnum moss sway in the breeze and leak their moisture into streams. Hidden waterfalls slap at granite boulders, spill into deep ravines, and finally fill valley rivers that flow back toward civilization.

Open Cockpit Barnstorming

above Dutchess County

High above the aerodrome, the atmosphere whines with the vibrations of tiny airborne motors. Under cirrus-streaked skies, you witness the aerial gymnastics of barnstorming antique planes. Then, with counterintuitive courage, adjust goggles and leather helmet while strapping yourself onto the worn cushions of a 1929 New Standard biplane. Throttling down a short grassy runway, your plane quickly approaches trees dead ahead; the wheezing propellers barely outrun a trailing haze of exhaust and smoky castor oil. Finally, wings grab the winds and climb reluctantly above the woods. Your safety is entrusted to a pilot steeped in World War I dogfighting skills, but like a mosquito caught in a gale, the small craft's canvas and wire framework bounces precariously on the airstream. The vintage bird suddenly vaults into tailsliding loops and wingovers, the deafening roar of the engine drowning out the screams of fellow passengers clutching this trackless rollercoaster. The pilot kills the switch, and you begin an earthbound plunge toward the peach orchards and estates of the Hudson River valley in a flight of fancy that your shaking legs won't let you soon forget.

Iceboating

along the Hudson River

Sprouting imaginatively from fairy tales and Hans Brinker's frozen Dutch canals, iceboats were an obsession for 19th-century Hudson Valley aristocrats who erected conspicuous mansions along the river's edge. With bowsprit and gaff-headed mainsail, these handsome yachts saluted the graceful lines of their sea-going cousins. Today, meticulously restored handcrafted wooden vessels whiz across the ice during the most bitter weeks of the year. Crawl under a thick bearskin throw and brace yourself within the oval tray shared with the skipper. Sailing at right angles to the wind, you fly over the crusty, tide-warped ice faster than the air currents clawing at the sail. At full tilt, sometimes just below 100 miles per hour, the spray of shaved ice pricks your cheeks and ferocious gusts yank tears off your lashes. Iceboating can be the coldest sport in the world. With a hand on the rudder and stiff attention paid to keeping the three sharpened runners from flickering out, it's possible to race a Manhattan-bound Amtrak on nearby rails.

DASHAWAY

All information is subject to change. Reserve or book as far ahead as you can. All organizations are open year-round unless otherwise noted.

CANOEING SWAMP TRAILS

North American Canoe Tours, Inc.
107 Camellia Street
Everglades City, FL 34139
Tel. 941/695-4666 or 941/395-3299
Fax 941/695-4155
(November–April)
Email: nact1@aol.com
www.evergladesadventures.com

Canoe and kayak rental for adventures in the Florida Everglades: $20–$55 per day. Guided tours: $40–$150 per day. NACT provides a 17-foot canoe, personal flotation devices and paddles for two, local maps, and seat cushions. Camping equipment rentals available; obtain permit for overnight camping from Gulf Coast or Flamingo Ranger Stations. Call the park service (tel. 941/695-3311) for more information and a backcountry trip planner. Trips available November–mid-April. MC, V, personal checks.

CANYONEERING

Bureau of Land Management Arizona Strip District Office
345 East Riverside Drive
St. George, UT 84790
Tel. 801/688-3230
Fax 801/688-3258
Email: j10wrigh@azblm.gov
www.for.nau.edu:80/paria-permits

BLM Paria Canyon–Vermilion Cliffs Wilderness
Kanab Resource Area
318 North First East
Kanab, UT 84741
Tel. 801/644-2672

Paria Canyon trail fee: $5 per person per day. Camping: $5 per site (up to five people per night). Hikers must obtain permits in advance and register at the trailhead (2 miles south of the Paria Information Station). The canyon is 37 miles long. Four days are recommended to make the hike from White House Trailhead to Lees Ferry. Hiking conditions change with the seasons. Be prepared for hiking in shallow water, quicksand, and crossing and recrossing the river. From July to September, flash floods are possible. Best times to visit: mid-March–June and October. No fires allowed. MC, V.

CATTLE DRIVING ROUNDUPS

Hargrave Cattle & Guest Ranch
Thompson River Valley
300 Thompson River Road
Marion, MN 59925
Tel. 406/858-2284 or 800/933-0696
Fax 406/858-2284
Email: hargrave@digisys.net
www.hargraveranch.com

Six-night stays: $1,050 May–mid-October, $700 mid-October–May, plus 10% service charge, all inclusive. Calving and branding March–May; cattle drives May–June; herd riding June–August; roundups September–mid-October. MC, V.

CLIMBING

Seneca Rocks Climbing School
Box 53
Seneca Rocks, WV 26884
Tel. 304/567-2600 or 800/548-0108
www.reston.com/senecaweb/school.html

Courses offered: Basic Rock Class (two or three days, $225–$275), Intermediate Rock Skills (three days, $300), Learning to Lead (two days, $250; three days $350), Private Guiding ($150), and group classes. All technical equipment provided. Programs available April–October (courses begin on Tuesdays and Saturdays). MC, V.

DOGSLEDDING

Boundary Country Trekking
7925 Gunflint Trail
Grand Marais, MN 55604
Tel. 218/388-4487 or 800/322-8327
Fax 218/388-4487
Email: bct@boreal.org
www.boreal.org/adventures/dogsled.html

Mushing adventures in Northern Minnesota's Boundary Waters Canoe Area Wilderness: two–four days $390–$1,090 per person; five–seven days $1,495–$1,725. Eight–fifteen days in the Canadian Northwest Territories: $2,800–$3,700 per person. All trips include lodging and meals. Trips available November–May. AE, MC, V, personal checks.

ENCOUNTERING POLAR BEARS

Tundra Buggy Tours
Box 662
Churchill, Manitoba
Canada R0B 0E0

Tel. 204/675–2121 or 800/544–5049
Fax 204/675–2877
(July–November)

Tel. 813/823–4026
Fax 813/894–2582
(December–June)

Half-day tours, full-day tours, and overnight stays on the frozen shores of the Hudson Bay: $59-$250 adults, $38-$250 children under 13, lunches, and transportation from hotel to Tundra Buggies. Three- or four-day tour packages from Winnepeg: $1,200-$2,600. Accommodations are provided in the Tundra Buggy Lodge, a 50-foot bunkhouse on wheels. Programs available July–November. MC, V.

HARP SEAL VIEWING

Natural Habitat Adventures
2945 Center Green Court, Suite H
Boulder, CO 80301
Tel. 303/449–3711 or 800/543–8917
Fax 303/449–3712
Email: nathab@worldnet.att.net
www.nathab.com

Five- to six-day adventures to Quebec's Magdalen Islands. Rates depend on length of stay and number of helicopter trips: $1,795–$3,295 per person based on double occupancy, plus breakfast, first and last nights' dinner and transportation, use of expedition suits and specialized equipment. $300 deposit required. Trips available mid-February–mid-March. AE, MC, V.

HELI-HIKING

CMH Heli-Hiking
Box 1660
Banff, Alberta
Canada T0L 0C0
Tel. 403/762–7100 or 800/661–0252
Fax 403/762–5879
http://199.183.146.20/cmh

One- to six-day adventures in the Canadian Rockies: CAN$191– CAN$2,680. Two or more nights include accommodation; all meals; helicopter flights; guide; equipment; transportation from Banff to Bugaboo, Bobbie Burns, and Adamants Lodges, and from Jasper for the two-night Cariboo Lodge holiday. Trips available July–August. MC, V, personal checks.

HIKING HUT TO HUT

Appalachian Mountain Club
Pinkham Notch Visitor Center
Rte. 16, Box 298
Gorham, NH 03581
Tel. 603/466–2721, ext. 195
Fax 603/466–2822
Email: tsteeves@amcinfo.org
www.outdoors.org

AMC Hut Reservations
Tel. 603/466–2727
Fax 603/466–3871

Huts are spaced along 56 miles of the Appalachian Trail in New Hampshire's White Mountains, one day's hike from each other. Huts are equipped with bunks, wool blankets, fresh water, lavatories, and a kitchen. Overnight lodging, $30–$62 for nonmembers, $23–$55 for members, including bunk, blanket, and 2 meals.

Guided hut-to-hut package: $220 per person, including transportation to trail-head, guiding services, two nights' lodging, dinners and breakfasts. Trips available June–September. MC, V.

HOT AIR BALLOONING

Balloon Federation of America
Box 400
Indianola, IA 50125
Tel. 515/961–8809
Fax 515/961–3735
Email: bfaoffice@aol.com
www.bfa.ycg.org

The BFA, a nonprofit organization, promotes ballooning and balloon safety and education. This organization is not an information service for hot-air ballon rides, but membership ($45/year) entitles you to publications that include upcoming international and national events. Contact event organizers to book a private balloon ascention.

HOUSEBOATING

Wahweap Lodge & Marina
Box 1597
Page, AZ 86040
Tel. 520/645–1111
Fax 520/645–1029

Wahweap Boat Rentals
Tel. 800/528–6154
Fax 602/331–5258
www.visitlakepowell.com

Three-day Lake Powell adventure: $800–$4,000. Houseboats vary in size, class, and amenities; rates are based on type of boat and length of trip (three–seven days). High season May–October. AE, D, DC, MC, V.

ICEBERG TRACKING

Twillingate Island Boat Tours Ltd.
The Iceberg Shop
Box 127
Twillingate, Newfoundland
Canada A0G 4M0
Tel. 709/884-2242 or 800/611-BERG
Fax 709/884-5575

Two-hour morning, afternoon, or evening tours off Twillingate Island: $25 per person. Programs available May–September. MC, V.

ICEBOATING

Hudson River Ice Yacht Club
Box 573
Rhinebeck, NY 12572
Tel. 914/876-6087
Email: MrIceboat@mhv.net

The yacht club provides information on ice and weather conditions. Membership to the club ($15) entitles you to a newsletter with information on locations of yachting rendezvous. Boats are not rented, but free rides are available upon request. Sailing season January–March. No credit cards.

LAND YACHTING

U.S. Manta Association
15618 E. Avenue Q7
Palmdale, CA 93591
Tel. 805/264-4270

Membership in the association ($10) entitles you to newsletters and information on land yachting. Boats are not rented, but free rides are available upon request. No credit cards.

LLAMA TREKKING

Windsong Llama Treks
1966 Martins Creek Road
Clyde, NC 28721
Tel. 704/627-6986
Email: sgord@primeline.com

Two- to three-day llama treks with camping in the Appalachians: $35–$100. Day trips and specialty treks (gourmet picnics, mountain biking, rock climbing, fly fishing) also available. Trips available March–November. D, MC, V.

MOUNTAIN BIKING

Moab Slickrock Bike Trail Rim Cyclery
94 West 100 North
Moab, UT 84532
Tel. 801/259-5333
Fax 801/259-7217
www.netoasis.com/rim

Bike rentals in Utah's red rock country: $28–$35 per day (less for three days or more), including water bottle and safety helmet. No guided tours. AE, D, MC, V.

OLYMPIC BOBSLEDDING

Olympic Sports Complex at Mt. Van Hoevenberg
Route 73
Lake Placid, NY 12946
Tel. 518/523-4436 or 800/462-6236
Fax 518/523-8203
www.orda.org

Half- and full-mile runs on Lake Placid's Mt. Van Hoevenberg: $30–$100 per person. Runs available mid-December–mid-March, Wednesday–Monday 10 am–4 pm (by reservation only). AE, D, MC, V.

OPEN COCKPIT BARNSTORMING

Old Rhinebeck Aerodrome
42 Stone Church Road
Rhinebeck, NY 12572
Tel. 914/758-8610
Fax 914/758-6481
www.mainstream.com/rhinebeck.html

Barnstorming rides (before and after airshows): $30 per person. Airshows 2 pm–4 pm: Monday–Friday $4 adults, $2 children 6–10; Saturday–Sunday $10 adults, $5 children 6–10. Weekend airshows mid-June–mid-October. MC, V.

PORTAGING

All Season's Outfitters
168 Lake Flower Avenue
Saranac Lake, NY 12983
Tel. 518/891-6159 or 800/236-5217

Canoe rentals for trips on New York State's Adirondack lakes: $25–$75 per day. All Season's Outfitters also offers guided trips and rentals of camping equipment. Trips available May–October. MC, V.

PUFFIN BIRDING

Sea Watch Tours
Box 48, Seal Cove
Grand Manan, New Brunswick
Canada E0G 3B0
Tel. 506/662-8552
Fax 506/662-1081
Email: beachfc@nbnet.nb.ca

Boat trip and landing on Machias Seal Island: $60. Boat trip only: $43 adults, $33 children 12–18, $23 children 6–11, free for children 5 and under, including tax. Trips available mid-June–August. MC, V, personal checks.

RACE CAR DRIVING

Bertil Roos IndyStyle Racing School
Box 221
Blakeslee, PA 18610
Tel. 717/646-7227 or 800/722-3669
Fax 717/646-4794
Email: roos@epix.net
www.racenow.com

Half- to five-day racing school: $395–$3,200, including suits, helmets, and safety gear. Programs available April–October. D, MC, V.

REENACTING HISTORIC BATTLES

Living History Association
Box 1389
Wilmington, VT 05363
Tel. 802/464-5569
www.quatron.com/lha/

Membership in the association entitles you to an annual events directory and newsletters listing local battle-reenactment organizations. Individual membership: $20 for one year, $55 for three years.

SPELUNKING

National Speleological Society
2813 Cave Avenue
Huntsville, AL 35810
Tel. 205/852-1300
Fax 205/851-9241
Email: nss@caves.org
www.caves.org

The NSS has numerous regional and local chapters that sponsor trips and offer training. Contact the national office for more information.

TALL SHIP SAILING

Sea Cloud
Cruise Company of Greenwich
Box 866
Norwalk, CT 06856
Tel. 203/852-0941 or 800/825-0826
Fax 203/852-0943
Email: 70752.2371@compuserve.com

One-week Caribbean cruise, double occupancy: $2,890–$6,620 excluding airfare. Accommodations on the *Sea Cloud* range from modern to original owner's suites and staterooms. Speak with officers on board about assisting with sail maneuvers. Personal checks only.

TORNADO CHASING

Cloud 9 Tours
1338 F Crown Point
Norman, OK 73072
Tel. 405/447-3171
Email: storms@pair.com
www3.pair.com/storms/cld9/cld9.html

Two-week chases in the Great Plains during peak tornado season, in May and June: $1,900, including lodging and ground transportation. $400 nonrefundable deposit. 18 years and up only. Cash or personal checks only.

WAGON TRAIN PIONEERING

Oregon Trail Wagon Train
Route 2, Box 502
Bayard, NE 69334
Tel. 308/586-1850
Fax 308/586-1848
Email: otwt@prairieweb.com
www.prairieweb.com/ot_wagon

Four- and six-day wagon train treks on the Nebraska prairies: $150–$579 adults, $125–$484 children under 12, including Continental breakfast the first morning and all subsequent pioneer-style meals on the trail. $50 per-person nonrefundable deposit required. Nightly Chuck Wagon cookouts: $17.95 adults, $9 children under 12. Trips available June–August. MC, V.

WHALE KISSING

Baja Expeditions Inc
Tel. 619/581-3311 or 800/843-6967
Fax 619/581-6542
Email: travel@bajaex.com
www.bajaex.com

Five- to ten-day whale watch expeditions in Baja California, Mexico: $995–$1,695 excluding airfare. Trips available January–mid-April. Personal checks or money orders.

WHITE-WATER RAFTING

Class VI River Runners
Box 78
Lansing, WV 25862
Tel. 304/574-0704 or 800/252-7784
Email: classvi@raftwv.com
www.raftwv.com

One-day rafting trip on West Virginia's New and Gauley rivers: $40–$180 per person, depending on the day of the week and level of difficulty. Multiday raft trips also available: $180–$325. Class VI River Runners also offers rentals of camping equipment, wetsuits, windbreakers, and surfjackets. Trips available April–October. AE, D, MC, V.